Copyright © 2016 by Jessica Henderson

Lime & Raisin Delightful Mug Cake

Total time: 6 mins

Servings: 2

Ingredients:

- ☐ A pinch of salt

- ☐ Zest of one lime

- ☐ 2 tbsperythritol

- ☐ 1 tsp baking powder

- ☐ 1/8 cup finely chopped raisins

- ☐ ¾ cup almond flour

- ☐ Juice of one lime

- ☐ 1 egg

- ☐ 2 tbsp butter

- ☐ ¼ cup powdered erythritol

Directions:

Keep the raisins aside and put all other ingredients in the food processor. Run the machine to make a smooth batter. Now, add the chopped raisins and distribute them evenly in the batter with a spoon.

Pour the batter in 2 microwave-safe mugs.Cook the cakes on high settings for 6 minutes and then let them cool down at room temperature before serving.

Nutrition per Serving

Protein: 7.5g

Fat: 4.3g

Carbohydrate: 6g Net

Nutty Pumpkin Magic Mug Cake

Total time: 7 mins

Servings: 1

Ingredients:

- ☐ 1 tbsp almond milk
- ☐ 2 tbsp pure pumpkin puree
- ☐ A pinch of salt
- ☐ ½ tsp pumpkin pie spice
- ☐ 1 tbsp ground flax seed
- ☐ 1 egg
- ☐ 1 tbsp coconut flour
- ☐ ¼ tsp baking powder
- ☐ 2 tbsp chopped almonds
- ☐ 1 tbsp chopped pistachio nuts
- ☐ ½ tsp vanilla flavoured liquid stevia
- ☐ ½ cup powdered erythritol

Directions:

Keep the chopped nuts aside and mix all the ingredients in a food processor to make the smooth batter.

Now, put the chopped nuts and use a spoon to distribute them evenly in the batter.

Pour the batter in a greased coffee mug and cook in the microwave oven on high setting for 7 minutes. Serve warm.

Nutrition per Serving

Protein: 9.5g

Fat: 7.6g

Carbohydrate: 2.4g Net

Almond Studded berry Delight in the Mug

Total time: 7 mins

Servings: 1

Ingredients:

- ½ cup almond flour
- ½ tsp baking powder
- ½ tsp cinnamon
- ½ cup mashed cranberries
- ¼ cup almonds, roughly chopped
- 1/8 tsp ground clove
- a pinch of salt
- 3 drops of stevia

Directions:

Keep the nuts aside and mix all other ingredients with a hand blender to make smooth batter.

Now, add the nuts and distribute them evenly in the batter with a spoon.Pour the batter in a greased coffee mug and cook in the microwave on high setting for 7 minutes.

Serve after slight cooling.

Nutrition per Serving

Protein: 32g

Fat: 5g

Carbohydrate: 3g Net

Pumpkin & Strawberry Majestic Mug Cake

Total time: 7 mins

Servings: 1

Ingredients:

- ½ cup almond milk

- ½ cup egg whites

- ½ cup almond flour

- ½ tsp baking powder

- A dash of salt

- ½ tsp cinnamon

- ½ cup mashed strawberries

- ¼ cup pumpkin puree

- 1/8 tsp pumpkin pie spice

- 3 drops stevia

Directions:

Put all the ingredients in a bowl with the help of an immersion blender and then pour the batter in an oven-safe mug.Cook in the microwave oven on high setting for 7 minutes and make sure that the top is brown in color.

Allow 5 minutes of standing time before serving.

Nutrition per Serving

Protein: 20g

Fat: 5g

Carbohydrate: 6g Net

Spicy Avocado Fantasy Mug

Total time: 5 mins

Servings: 1

Ingredients:

- ☐ ½ cup almond flour

- ☐ ½ tsp baking powder

- ☐ A dash of salt

- ☐ ½ cup almond milk

- ☐ ½ cup egg whites

- ☐ ½ tsp cinnamon

- ☐ 1 ripe avocado, diced

- ☐ 3 drops stevia

Directions:

Keep the avocado pieces aside and blend all other ingredients with a hand blender to make smooth batter.

Now add the avocado pieces and distribute them evenly in the batter with a spoon.

Pour the batter in a coffee mug and cook in microwave oven for 5 minutes. Bring the cake to room temperature before serving.

Nutrition per Serving

Protein: 20g

Fat: 5g

Carbohydrate: 6g Net

Creamy Delightful Lemon Mug Cake

Total time: 5 mins

Servings: 1

Ingredients:

- ☐ 1 cup erythritol
- ☐ ½ cup almond flour
- ☐ 1 tbsplemon zest
- ☐ 1 cup lemon puree
- ☐ ½ cup almond cream
- ☐ 1 large egg
- ☐ 2 tbsp almond butter

Directions:

Put all the ingredients in a big bowl and use an immersion blender to make smooth batter.

Pour the batter into a greased coffee mug and cook in microwave for 5 minutes. Let it sit in the oven for some time and then bring out the cake.

Serve after bringing the cake at room temperature.

Nutrition per Serving

Protein: 3g

Fat: 9g

Carbohydrate: 3.6g Net

Orange & Raspberry Fantastic Duo

Total time: 25 mins

Servings: 6

Ingredients:

- □ ½ tsporange zest

- □ 5 packets of stevia

- □ ½ tsp baking soda

- □ 2 eggs

- □ 1/8 cup melted butter

- □ ¼ tsp salt

- □ 1 cup heavy cream

- □ 2 cups almond flour

- □ ½ tsporange extract

- □ 4 oz fresh raspberries (mashed)

Directions:

Keep the oven ready by preheating it at 350 degrees and grease 6 oven-safe mugs.Reserve some whole raspberries, and two tea spoons of heavy cream for garnishing.

Blend the wet and dry ingredients separately and then blend them together with a hand blender to make the smooth batter.

Pour the batter into the mugs and bake the cakes for 20 minutes. Let them stand in the oven for another 5 minutes and then allow complete cooling. Garnish the cakes with the heavy cream and reserved berries.

Nutrition per Serving

Protein: 5g

Fat: 17g

Carbohydrate: 6g Net

Creamy & Nutty Berry Magic

Total time: 20 mins

Servings: 6

Ingredients:

- 1½ cup chopped almonds

- ½ tsp xanthan gum

- 2 tsp baking powder

- ½ cup flax seed meal

- 3 eggs

- ½ tsp salt

- 1/3 cup water

- 1 cup Strawberries, chopped

- ½ cup butter

- ¼ cup heavy cream

- 1/3 cup erythritol

- 1/3 cup water

Directions:

Keep the almonds and strawberries aside and then mix the wet and dry ingredients in separate bowls.

Blend them together with an immersion blender to make the smooth batter. Now, put the almonds and strawberries into the batter and use a spoon to distribute them evenly. Remember to reserve some berries and nuts for final topping.

Pour the batter in 6 greased oven-safe mugs and make the topping with the nuts and berries.

Bake the cakes at 350 degrees for 17 minutes and let them stand in the oven for another 3 minutes.

Allow 5 minutes of standing time and then serve.

Nutrition per Serving

Protein: 3.9g

Fat: 8g

Carbohydrate: 1.6g Net

Herb Filled Cheesy Mug Cake

Total time: 30 mins

Servings: 6

Ingredients:

- [ ] 3 tbsp unsweetened almond milk
- [ ] 16 drops of stevia extract
- [ ] 2 tsp molasses
- [ ] 1½ cup almond flour
- [ ] 2 large eggs
- [ ] 8 oz cream cheese
- [ ] 3 oz mozzarella cheese
- [ ] ¼ cup erythritol
- [ ] ¼ cup whey protein powder
- [ ] ¼ cup chopped basil leaves
- [ ] 2 tsp baking powder
- [ ] ½ tsp baking soda
- [ ] 1 tsp ground cinnamon

- ¼ tsp salt

- ½ tsp ground cloves

- 1 tsp finely chopped basil, for garnishing

- 1oz heavy cream, for garnishing

Directions:

Keep the basil leaves aside. Blend the wet and dry ingredients in separate bowls and then blend them together with an immersion blender to make the cake batter. Now, add the basil leaves and distribute them evenly in the batter with a spoon.

Pour the batter in 6 oven-safe mugs and bake the cakes at 325 degrees for 25 minutes. Let them stand in the oven for 5 minutes and then allow complete cooling before taking them out from the mugs.

Serve by garnishing with heavy cream and freshly minced basil leaves.

Nutrition per Serving

Protein: 3.9g

Fat: 2g

Carbohydrate: 6.9g Net

Nutty Chocolate Cakes With Coffee Glaze

Total time: 35 mins

Servings: 5

Ingredients for making nutty mug cakes:

- ½ tsp baking soda

- ¼ cup whey protein powder

- ¼ cup erythritol

- 2 tsp baking powder

- ½ tsp salt

- 4 oz sour cream

- 16 drops of stevia extract

- 1¼ cup Almonds, chopped

- 1 cups almond flour

- 1 tsp dark chocolate powder

- ¼ cup butter

- 3 large eggs

- 2 tbsp almond milk

Ingredients for making the glaze:

☐   1/3 cup powdered erythritol

☐   2 tbsp strong coffee

Directions:

Keep the chopped almonds aside and then mix the wet and dry ingredients separately. Now blend them together by using a hand blender to make the smooth batter. Put the chopped almonds in the batter and use a spoon to distribute them evenly in the batter.

Pour the batter in 5 greased oven-safe mugs and bake the cakes at 325 degrees for 27 minutes. Let the cakes stand in the oven for 5 minutes. Allow cooling before taking out the cakes from the mugs.

Now, make the coffee glaze by mixing the strong coffee with erythritol and spread the mixture over the cakes. Keep in fridge for 10 minutes so that the glaze coating can set properly.

Nutrition per Serving

Protein: 3.9g

Fat: 2g

Carbohydrate: 7.9g Net

Chocolate Glazed Coconut Delight Mug Cake

Total time: 35 mins

Servings: 5

Ingredients for making the cake:

- [ ] 2 tsp baking powder
- [ ] ½ tsp baking soda
- [ ] ¼ cup whey protein powder
- [ ] 3 tbsp coconut oil
- [ ] 1½ cups of coconut flakes
- [ ] ½ tsp salt
- [ ] 4 oz cream cheese
- [ ] 16 drops of stevia extract
- [ ] ¼ cup coconut milk
- [ ] 2 large eggs
- [ ] 2 cups almond flour
- [ ] ¼ cup erythritol

☐   ½ tsp vanilla extract

Ingredients for making the chocolate glaze:

☐   1/3 cup powdered erythritol

☐   1 tbsp dark chocolate

Directions:

Keep the shredded coconut aside and then mix the wet and dry ingredients in separate bowls. Use a hand blender to blend the wet and dry ingredients to make a smooth batter. Now, put the shredded coconut and use a spoon to distribute them evenly in the batter.

Coat 5 oven-safe mugs with cooking spray and pour the batter in the mugs. Bake the cakes for 27 minutes at 325 degrees and then let the cakes rest in the oven for another 5 minutes. Allow complete cooling and then take out the cakes from the mugs.

Make the chocolate glaze by mixing the ingredients and spread the mixture over the mug cakes. Keep in fridge for some time so that the glaze coating can set properly.

Nutrition per Serving

Protein: 3.9g

Fat: 2g

Carbohydrate: 3.8g Net

Spicy Fruit Cakes With Orange glaze

Total time: 35 mins

Servings: 5

Ingredients for spicy mug cakes:

- ¼ cup whey protein powder

- ½ tsp baking soda

- 2 tsp baking powder

- 4 oz cream cheese

- ½ tsp salt

- ¼ cup granulated erythritol

- 2 cups of almond flour

- ¼ cup almond milk

- 1 tbsp garam masala

- 2 large eggs

- ¼ cup butter

- 24 drops of stevia extract

- 1/8 cup chopped raisins

☐   1/8 cup chopped apples

Ingredients for making orange glaze:

☐   1 tbsp orange juice

☐   ¼ cup powdered erythritol

Directions:

Keep raisins and apples aside and then mix the wet and dry ingredients in separate bowls and then blend them together to make the cake batter. Now, add the raisins and apples into the batter and distribute them evenly with a spoon.

Pour the batter in 5 greased oven-safe mugs and bake them at 325 degrees for 27 minutes. Allow complete cooling after baking.

In the meantime, make the orange glaze by mixing the orange juice with erythritol.

Bring out the cakes from the mugs and then spread the orange glaze on top. Keep in fridge for a few minutes so that the glaze coating can set properly.

Nutrition per Serving

Protein: 3.9g

Fat: 2g

Carbohydrate: 3.9g Net

Delightful Spicy Pumpkin Cakes with Chocolate Glaze

Total time: 35 mins

Servings: 5

Ingredients for spicy mug cakes:

- ¼ cup whey protein powder

- ½ tsp baking soda

- 2 tsp baking powder

- 4 oz cream cheese

- ½ tsp salt

- ¼ cup granulated erythritol

- 2 cups of almond flour

- ¼ cup almond milk

- 1 tbsp pumpkin pie spice

- 2 large eggs

- ¼ cup butter

- 24 drops of stevia extract

☐ ½ cup pumpkin puree

Ingredients for making chocolate glaze:

☐ 1 tsp dark chocolate

☐ 2 tsp melted butter

☐ ¼ cup powdered erythritol

Directions:

Mix all the wet and dry ingredients in separate bowls and then blend them together to make the cake batter.

Pour the batter in 5 greased oven-safe mugs and bake them at 325 degrees for 27 minutes. Allow complete cooling after baking.

In the meantime, make the chocolate glaze by mixing the chocolate powder with butter and erythritol.

Bring out the cakes from the mugs and then spread the chocolate glaze on top. Keep in fridge for a few minutes so that the glaze coating can set properly.

Nutrition per Serving

Protein: 3.9g

Fat: 2g

Carbohydrate: 3.9g Net

Nut Filled Apple Mug Cakes

Total time: 40 mins

Servings: 6

Ingredients:

- ☐ 1/3 cup whey protein powder
- ☐ 1 tsp ground cinnamon
- ☐ ¼ tsp ground cloves
- ☐ 2 cups almond flour
- ☐ 2 cups mashed apples
- ☐ ½ tsp salt
- ☐ 1/3 cup erythritol
- ☐ 2 tsp baking powder
- ☐ ½ tsp baking soda
- ☐ ½ tsp ground ginger
- ☐ ¼ cup almond milk
- ☐ ½ cup chopped walnuts
- ☐ ¼ cup coconut oil

- ☐ 1/3 cup Greek yogurt

- ☐ 1/8 tsp salt

- ☐ 2 large eggs

- ☐ ¼ tsp liquid stevia extract

- ☐ ½ tsp vanilla extract

Directions:

Keep the mashed apples and walnuts aside and then mix the wet and dry ingredients in separate bowls and blend them together to make the batter. Add mashed apples and walnuts to this batter and whisk with a spoon to blend the apples well with the batter.

Pour the batter in 6 greased oven-safe mugs and bake the cakes at 325 degrees for 35 minutes, making sure that the top of the cakes turn golden brown in color.

Allow 5 minutes standing time in the oven and then cool them completely before taking the cakes out of the mugs. Serve by garnishing with some heavy cream.

Nutrition per Serving

Protein: 3.9g

Fat: 2g

Carbohydrate: 3.8g Net

Spiral Spaghetti Squash Cakes Infused With Almonds

Total time: 40 mins

Servings: 6

Ingredients:

- ☐ 1/3 cup whey protein powder

- ☐ 1 tsp ground cinnamon

- ☐ ¼ tsp ground cloves

- ☐ 2 cups almond flour

- ☐ 2 cups sprialized spaghetti squash

- ☐ ½ tsp salt

- ☐ 1/3 cup erythritol

- ☐ 2 tsp baking powder

- ☐ ½ tsp baking soda

- ☐ ½ tsp ground ginger

- ☐ ¼ cup almond milk

- ☐ ½ cup chopped almonds

- ☐ ¼ cup coconut oil

- ☐ 1/3 cup Greek yogurt

- ☐ 1/8 tsp salt

- ☐ 2 large eggs

- ☐ ¼ tsp liquid stevia extract

- ☐ ½ tsp vanilla extract

Directions:

Keep the spaghetti squash and almonds aside and then mix the wet and dry ingredients in separate bowls and blend them together to make the batter. Add squash and almonds to this batter and whisk with a spoon to blend them well with the batter.

Pour the batter in 6 greased oven-safe mugs and bake the cakes at 325 degrees for 35 minutes, making sure that the top of the cakes turn golden brown in color.

Allow 5 minutes standing time in the oven and then cool them completely before taking the cakes out of the mugs. Serve by garnishing with some heavy cream.

Nutrition per Serving

Protein: 3.9g

Fat: 2g

Carbohydrate: 3.8g Net

Simple Nuts & Raisins Mug Cake

Total time: 35 mins

Servings: 6

Ingredients:

- ½ cup softened butter

- 1/3 cup whey protein powder

- 1/8 cup chopped walnuts

- 1/8 cup chopped pistachio nuts

- 1/8 cup chopped raisins

- 2 tbsp almond slices, for topping

- ½ tsp salt

- 3 cups of almond flour

- 1½ tsp baking powder

- 1 tsp baking soda

- 1 tsp almond extract

- 3 large eggs

- 20 drops of stevia extract

☐ ½ cup almond milk

☐ ½ cup erythritol

Directions:

Make the mixture of whey protein powder, baking soda, baking powder, salt and almond flour and keep it aside.

Put all the wet ingredients in a bowl and use a hand blender to blend them. Now, blend in the dry mixture and make use of the hand blender to make the cake batter. Add chopped nuts and raisins and distribute them evenly in the batter with a spoon.

Pour the batter in 6 oven-safe mugs and top the batter with slices of almond.

Bake the cakes at 325 degrees for 30 minutes and let them stand in the oven for another 5 minutes.

Allow complete cooling and then serve.

Nutrition per Serving

Protein: 6g

Fat: 7.9g

Carbohydrate: 5.5g Net

Hot & Cheesy Magical Mug Cake

Total time: 30 mins

Servings: 6

Ingredients:

- ☐ 1½ tsp baking powder

- ☐ 1 tsp baking soda

- ☐ ½ tsp salt

- ☐ ½ tsp xanthan gum

- ☐ 1/3 cup pickled jalapenos

- ☐ ¼ tsp hot sauce

- ☐ 1½ cup mozzarella cheese

- ☐ ¼ cup almond milk

- ☐ ¼ cup olive oil

- ☐ ½ tsp marinara sauce

- ☐ 1 tsp Dijon mustard

- ☐ ½ cup flax seed meal

- ☐ 2 cups almond flour

□   4 large eggs

Directions:

Mix wet and dry ingredients separately and then blend them together with a hand blender to make the smooth batter

Pour the batter in 6 oven-safe mugs and bake the cakes at 350 degrees for 25 minutes. Allow 5 minutes of standing time in the oven and then let the cakes cool down completely. Bring out the cakes from the mugs and garnish with some more mustard and hot sauce.

Nutrition per Serving

Protein: 3g

Fat: 4.5g

Carbohydrate: 3g Net

Simplest Ever Choco-Nutty Mug Cake

Total time: 30 mins

Servings: 6

Ingredients:

- ☐ 1 cup coconut flour

- ☐ 2.5 oz dark chocolate

- ☐ 1 tbsp molasses

- ☐ 1 cup walnuts, chopped

- ☐ A pinch of salt

- ☐ ¾ cup erythritol

- ☐ 2 large eggs

- ☐ ½ cup melted butter

Directions:

Keep the nuts aside and put all other ingredients in a bowl. Use a hand blender to make the smooth batter and then add the chopped nuts. Distribute them evenly in the batter with a spoon.

Pour the batter into 6 small mugs and then spread some more chopped walnuts on top.

Bake the cakes at 325 degrees for 25 minutes, making sure that the top of the cakes are golden brown in color.

Allow 5 minutes standing time in the oven and then cool them completely before taking out from the mugs.

Nutrition per Serving

Protein: 1.5g

Fat: 9.2g

Carbohydrate: 3.3g Net

Creamy Pumpkin Cakes with Goodness of Cheese

Total time: 40 mins

Servings: 8

Ingredients:

- ☐ 3 cups of almond flour
- ☐ ½ tsp baking soda
- ☐ ¼ cup almond milk
- ☐ ½ tsp vanilla extract
- ☐ 1/3 cup whey protein powder
- ☐ ½ tsp salt
- ☐ ½ tsp ginger
- ☐ 1½ tsp cinnamon
- ☐ 1/8 cup heavy cream
- ☐ ½ cup cheddar cheese
- ☐ ¼ tsp cloves
- ☐ ¾ cup pumpkin puree

- ☐ 2 tsp baking powder

- ☐ 3 large eggs

- ☐ ½ cup erythritol

Directions:

Mix the wet and dry ingredients in separate bowls and then blend them together to make the batter. Use a hand blender to make the batter smooth.

Grease 8 small mugs with cooking spray and then pour the batter into the mugs. Bake the cakes at 325 degrees for 35 minutes and then allow standing in the oven for another 5 minutes.

Serve warm.

Nutrition per Serving

Protein: 9g

Fat: 22g

Carbohydrate: 4g Net

Orange Studded Choco-Nutty Cakes

Total time: 25 mins

Servings: 6

Ingredients:

- ☐ 3 oz dark chocolate chips

- ☐ ¼ tsp salt

- ☐ ¾ cup erythritol

- ☐ 1 tbsp baking powder

- ☐ 6 large eggs

- ☐ ½ cup almond milk

- ☐ 1/3 cup coconut oil

- ☐ ½ cup whole orange, diced

- ☐ ¾ cup almond flour

- ☐ ¼ cup finely chopped almonds

- ☐ 1 tsp vanilla extract

Directions:

Keep chocolate chips, almonds, and orange pieces aside and then mix the wet and dry ingredients separately. Use a hand blender to make the batter smooth. Now, mix the orange, almonds, and chocolate chips with the batter and use a spoon to distribute them evenly in the batter.

Pour the batter in greased oven-safe mugs and bake the cakes at 350 degrees for 20 minutes and let them stand in the oven for next 5 minutes. Serve after complete cooling.

Nutrition per Serving

Protein: 6g

Fat: 15g

Carbohydrate: 6g Net

Fiery Tomato Mug Cake

Total time: 35 mins

Servings: 6

Ingredients:

- [ ] 1/3 cup erythritol
- [ ] 1 cup coconut flour
- [ ] ½ tsp salt
- [ ] 1 tbsp baking powder
- [ ] 1 cup almond milk
- [ ] 7 large eggs
- [ ] ½ tsp vanilla
- [ ] 1/25 cup butter
- [ ] 3 tbsp minced jalapeno peppers
- [ ] 1 cup tomato puree
- [ ] 1 jalapeno for garnishing, thinly sliced

Directions:

Blend the coconut flour with erythritol, salt and baking powder and then beat in the eggs along with melted butter, vanilla, tomato puree, and almond milk. Use a hand blender to make the batter smooth. Now add the jalapeno pieces, distribute them evenly and pour the batter into 6 oven-safe mugs.

Bake the cakes at 325 degrees for 30 minutes and allow 5 minutes of standing time in the oven. Let the cakes cool down completely and then bring them out from the mugs. Garnish with some jalapeno slices.

Nutrition per Serving

Protein: 5.21g

Fat: 11.22g

Carbohydrate: 7.08g Net

Majestic Coconut-Walnut Mug Cakes

Total time: 35 mins

Servings: 5

Ingredients for coconut mug cake batter:

- [ ] 1/3 cup whey protein

- [ ] ¼ tsp salt

- [ ] 2 large eggs

- [ ] 1/3 cup shredded coconut

- [ ] ½ tbsp baking powder

- [ ] ½ cup softened butter

- [ ] ¼ cup erythritol

- [ ] 1 cup almond milk

- [ ] ½ cup cocoa powder

- [ ] 2/3 cup coconut flour

- [ ] 1 tsp coconut extract

Ingredients for walnut topping:

- [ ] 2 tbsp butter

- ½ cup chocolate chips (sugar free)

- 1/3 cup coconut flakes

- 1/3 cup finely chopped walnuts

Directions:

Mix the wet and dry ingredients in separate bowls and then blend them together to make the smooth batter for mug cakes.

Pour the batter in 5 medium sized oven-safe mugs and bake them at 325 degrees for 20 minutes. Once baked, keep aside for complete cooling.

Melt the chocolate in a double boiler and mix it with the butter. Spread the mixture over the mug cakes and top with the coconut flakes and chopped walnuts. Keep the cakes in fridge for some time so that the topping can set properly.

Nutrition per Serving

Protein: 5.7g

Fat: 20.1g

Carbohydrate: 5.28g Net

Cheesy Tomato Mug Cakes

Total time: 35 mins

Servings: 6

Ingredients:

- ☐ 2 cups tomato puree

- ☐ ½ cup diced tomatoes

- ☐ ¼ tsp salt

- ☐ 1/3 cup coconut flour

- ☐ 2½ baking powder

- ☐ 3 large eggs

- ☐ 1 cup crumbled feta cheese

- ☐ ½ cup almond milk

- ☐ 1/3 cup whey protein

- ☐ 2 cups almond flour

- ☐ ½ tsp garlic powder

- ☐ 1 tsp dried oregano

- ☐ ½ tsp onion powder

☐ ¼ tsp pepper

☐ ¼ cup melted butter

Directions:

Preheat the oven at 325 degrees and grease 6 oven-safe mugs with cooking spray. Pour all the ingredients except tomato dices in a mixing bowl and use a hand blender to make smooth batter. Add diced tomatoes and distribute them evenly with a spoon.

Pour the batter into the greased mugs and bake in the oven for 30 minutes. Allow 5 minutes of resting time before serving.

Nutrition per Serving

Protein: 2.91g

Fat: 13.8g

Carbohydrate: 6.73g Net

Delightful Zucchini Cakes with Lots of Cheese

Total time: 35 mins

Servings: 6

Ingredients:

- 2½ cups shredded zucchini
- ¼ tsp salt
- 1/3 cup coconut flour
- 2½ baking powder
- 3 large eggs
- 1 cup crumbled feta cheese
- ¼ cup mozzarella cheese
- ½ cup almond milk
- 1/3 cup whey protein
- 2 cups almond flour
- ½ tsp garlic powder
- 1 tsp dried oregano

- ☐ ½ tsp onion powder

- ☐ ¼ tsp pepper

- ☐ ¼ cup melted butter

Directions:

Preheat the oven at 325 degrees and grease 6 oven-safe mugs with cooking spray.

Keep the shredded zucchini in a sieve and sprinkle some salt over it. This will help in bringing out the excess moisture from the vegetable.

Now, put all the ingredientsin a mixing bowl and use a hand blender to make smooth batter.

Pour the batter into the greased mugs and bake in the oven for 30 minutes. Allow 5 minutes of resting time before serving.

Nutrition per Serving

Protein: 2.91g

Fat: 13.8g

Carbohydrate: 6.73g Net

Coconut & Orange Cakes with Punch of Dark Chocolate

Total time: 15 mins

Servings: 6

Ingredients:

- ☐ 2 large eggs
- ☐ 1 tsp baking soda
- ☐ 2 tbsp cocoa powder
- ☐ 6 tbsp water
- ☐ ¼ cup shredded coconut
- ☐ ½ tsp vanilla extract
- ☐ ¼ cup erythritol
- ☐ 1 cup melted butter
- ☐ 1 whole orange, mashed
- ☐ ¼ cup chocolate chips

Directions:

Add the melted butter with mashed orange, water and eggs in the blender to make smooth mixture. Add the baking soda, erythritol, vanilla extract, shredded coconut, and cocoa powder with this mixture to make the batter for mug cakes. Add the chocolate chips and distribute them evenly with a spoon.

Now, pour the batter into 6 mugs and bake them for 12 minutes at 350 degrees. Keep the mugs in the oven for another 2 minutes and then serve by garnishing with some cream of your choice.

Nutrition per Serving

Protein: 7g

Fat: 12.6g

Carbohydrate: 7.7g Net

Coconut & Mango Splendor Mug Cake

Total time: 15 mins

Servings: 6

Ingredients:

- 6 tbsp water

- 2 large eggs

- 1 tsp baking soda

- ½ tsp vanilla extract

- ¼ cup erythritol

- 1 cup melted butter

- 1 ripe mango, mashed

- ¼ cup shredded coconut

Directions:

Keep shredded coconut aside and put all other ingredients in a large mixing bowl. Use a hand blender to make a smooth batter. Now, add the shredded coconut and distribute them evenly with a spoon.

Pour the batter into 6 mugs and bake them for 12 minutes at 350 degrees. Keep the mugs in the oven for another 2 minutes and then garnish with some heavy cream and shredded coconut.

Nutrition per Serving

Protein: 7g

Fat: 12.6g

Carbohydrate: 7.7g Net

Mango & Pistachio Overwhelming Mug Cakes

Total time: 40 mins

Servings: 5

Ingredients:

- ½ cup almond milk

- 1 large ripe mango, mashed

- 2 cups almond flour

- ¼ cup melted butter

- 2 tbsp chia seeds

- ¼ cup coconut oil

- 4 large eggs (separated)

- 1 tsp baking soda

- 2/3 cup finely chopped pistachio

- 15 drops of liquid stevia

- ¼ tsp salt

- 2 tsp cream of tartar

☐   ½ cup erythritol

Directions:

Begin by beating the egg yolks in a bowl and then add the butter, erythritol and stevia to make a creamy mixture. Add mashed mango, almond flour, chia seeds, baking soda, and salt to it and beat thoroughly.

Beat the egg whites with the cream of tartar till soft peaks are formed and then incorporate this mixture with the egg yolk mixture.

Pour the batter into greased mugs and bake them in the preheated oven at 350 degrees for 30 minutes. The top of the cakes has to be golden brown in color. Allow 10 minutes standing time in the oven and then use a knife to take out the cakes from the mug.

Nutrition per Serving

Protein: 6.9g

Fat: 18.6g

Carbohydrate: 4.2g Net

Bacon & Tomato Delightful Mug Cake

Total time: 30 mins

Servings: 8

Ingredients:

- ☐　1 tsp psyllium husk powder
- ☐　1/8 cup flaxseed meal
- ☐　3 slices of bacon (crisped and crumbled)
- ☐　2.5oz Cheddar cheese
- ☐　2 medium ripe tomatoes, diced
- ☐　1½　medium spring onions
- ☐　1 tsp dried cilantro
- ☐　3 eggs
- ☐　1/4 cup almond flour
- ☐　2 tbsp butter
- ☐　Salt and pepper
- ☐　½ tsp baking powder
- ☐　1tbsp lemon juice

- □ ½ tsp minced garlic

- □ ½ tsp dried chives

- □ 1/8 tsp red chilli flakes

- □ 1 cup coconut milk

Directions:

Begin by beating the eggs and then mix almond flour, flaxseed meal, psyllium husk powder, coconut milk and lemon juice with it. Keep this mixture aside.

Cook the crisped bacon with butter for a minute along with diced tomatoes and spring onion. Now, add cilantro, garlic, chives, chilli flakes, salt, and pepper. Sauté the ingredients till they become fragrant.   Blend them with the egg mixture to make the cake batter.

Pour the batter into 8 small mugs and cook in microwave oven for 30 minutes. The top of the cake must be golden brown in color.

Nutrition per Serving

Protein: 6.1g

Fat: 14.1g

Carbohydrate: 1.5g Net

Healthy Spinach & Bacon Mug Cake

Total time: 30 mins

Servings: 8

Ingredients:

- ☐ 1 tsp psyllium husk powder
- ☐ 1/8 cup flaxseed meal
- ☐ 3 slices of bacon (crisped and crumbled)
- ☐ 2.5oz Cheddar cheese
- ☐ 2 cups spinach leaves (boiled)
- ☐ 1½ medium spring onions
- ☐ 1 tsp dried cilantro
- ☐ 3 eggs
- ☐ 1/4 cup almond flour
- ☐ 2 tbsp butter
- ☐ Salt and pepper
- ☐ ½ tsp baking powder
- ☐ 1tbsp lemon juice

- ½ tsp minced garlic

- ½ tsp dried chives

- 1/8 tsp red chilli flakes

- 1 cup coconut milk

Directions:

Begin by beating the eggs and then mix almond flour, flaxseed meal, psyllium husk powder, coconut milk and lemon juice with it. Keep this mixture aside.

Cook the crisped bacon with butter for a minute along with boiled spinach leaves and spring onion. Now, add cilantro, garlic, chives, chilli flakes, salt, and pepper. Sauté the ingredients till they become fragrant. Blend them with the egg mixture to make the cake batter.

Pour the batter into 8 small mugs and cook in microwave oven for 30 minutes. The top of the cake must be golden brown in color.

Nutrition per Serving

Protein: 6.1g

Fat: 14.1g

Carbohydrate: 1.5g Net

Vanilla Flavored Chicken Cakes

Total time: 30 mins

Servings: 6

Ingredients:

- 1 cup of almond flour
- 3oz minced chicken, cooked
- 2 large eggs
- 1 tsp vanilla flavoring
- 2tbsp coconut milk
- 1tbsppsyllium husk powder
- 1/8tsp salt
- ½ tsp baking powder
- ¼ cup erythritol
- 10 drops of stevia

Directions:

Mix the wet and dry ingredients in two separate bowls and then blend them together to make the batter. Remember to add the cooked chicken at the end.

Pour the batter into 6 small microwave safe mugs and cook in microwave oven for 30 minutes. Let the cakes rest in the oven for 5 minutes and then serve.

Nutrition per Serving

Protein: 7.8g

Fat: 13.3g

Carbohydrate: 2.1g Net

Maple Flavored Walnut Magic Mug Cake

Total time: 35 mins

Servings: 5

Ingredients:

- ¼ cup walnuts, coarsely chopped
- ½ cup almond flour
- ½ cup flaxseed
- 2 large eggs
- ½ tsp baking soda
- ¼ cup erythritol
- 1 tsp vanilla extract
- ¼ tsp liquid stevia
- ½ cup coconut oil
- 2 tsp maple extract
- ½ tsp apple cider vinegar

Directions:

Reserve one-third portion of chopped walnuts for final topping.

Blend the wet and dry ingredients in separate bowls and then blend them together to make the batter. Pour the batter in 5 small mugs and then make the final topping with the reserved walnuts.

Cook the cakes in microwave oven for 30 minutes, making sure that the cake is well set. Allow 5 minutes of resting time in the oven and serve after cooling.

Nutrition per Serving

Protein: 4.8g

Fat: 20.7g

Carbohydrate: 1.5g Net

Apple-Maple Majestic Mug Cake

Total time: 35 mins

Servings: 5

Ingredients:

- 1 cup apples, chopped into small cubes
- ½ cup almond flour
- ½ cup flaxseed
- 2 large eggs
- ½ tsp baking soda
- ¼ tsp liquid stevia
- ½ cup coconut oil
- ¼ cup erythritol
- 1 tsp vanilla extract
- 2 tsp maple extract
- ½ tsp apple cider vinegar

Directions:

Reserveone-third portion of chopped apples for the final topping.

Blend the wet and dry ingredients in separate bowls and then blend them together to make the batter. The chopped apples are to be added at the end and distributed evenly with a spoon. Pour the batter in 5 small mugs and then make the final topping with the reserved apple cubes.

Cook the cakes in microwave oven for 30 minutes, making sure that the cake is well set. Allow 5 minutes of standing time in the oven and serve after cooling.

Nutrition per Serving

Protein: 4.8g

Fat: 20.7g

Carbohydrate: 1.5g Net

Spicy Nut Filled Cake

Total time: 35 mins

Servings: 6

Ingredients:

- ☐ ¼ cup heavy cream
- ☐ 1/8 cup peanut butter
- ☐ 1tbsp coconut oil
- ☐ ¼ cup almond flour
- ☐ 3 large eggs
- ☐ 1/8 cup toasted walnuts
- ☐ ½ tbsp unsalted butter
- ☐ 1/8 tsp nutmeg
- ☐ 1/8 tsp salt
- ☐ 5 drops of liquid stevia
- ☐ ½ tsp cinnamon
- ☐ 1tbsperythritol
- ☐ ½ tsp vanilla

Directions:

Make a mixture of erythritol, nutmeg, and salt and keep it aside.

Mix all the wet ingredients together and then blend the dry mixture with it to make the batter. Add the roasted almonds at the end and pour the batter in 6 small mugs.

Cook them in microwave oven for 30 minutes and allow some standing time in the oven.

These mug cakes can be served as evening snacks.

Nutrition per Serving

Protein: 6.9g

Fat: 16.3g

Carbohydrate: 2g Net

Hazelnut Splendora with Maple Delight

Total time: 35 mins

Servings: 6

Ingredients:

- ☐ 3 large eggs
- ☐ ¼ cup heavy cream
- ☐ 1/8 cup peanut butter
- ☐ 1tbsp coconut oil
- ☐ 1tbsperythritol
- ☐ ¼ cup almond flour
- ☐ ½ tsp vanilla
- ☐ 1/8 cup maple syrup
- ☐ 1/8 tsp salt
- ☐ 5 drops of liquid stevia
- ☐ 1/8 cup chopped hazel nuts
- ☐ ½ tbsp unsalted butter
- ☐ ½ tsp cinnamon

Directions:

Blend the dry ingredients and wet ingredients separately and then blend them together to make the batter. Add the hazel nuts at the end.

Pour the batter in 6 small mugs and cook them in microwave oven for 30 minutes. Let the cakes rest in the oven for 5 minutes and then allow complete cooling before taking them out from the mugs. Garnish with heavy cream.

Nutrition per Serving

Protein: 6.9g

Fat: 16.3g

Carbohydrate: 2g Net

Pecan Splendora with Bliss of Honey

Total time: 35 mins

Servings: 6

Ingredients:

- ☐ 3 large eggs
- ☐ ¼ cup heavy cream
- ☐ 1/8 cup peanut butter
- ☐ 1tbsp coconut oil
- ☐ 8 tbsp honey
- ☐ ¼ cup almond flour
- ☐ ½ tsp vanilla
- ☐ 1/8 tsp salt
- ☐ 5 drops of liquid stevia
- ☐ 1/8 cup chopped pecans
- ☐ ½ tbsp unsalted butter
- ☐ ½ tsp cinnamon

Directions:

Blend the dry ingredients and wet ingredients separately and then blend them together to make the batter. Add the pecans at the end.

Pour the batter in 6 small mugs and make the topping with some chopped pecans. Cook the cakes in microwave oven for 30 minutes. Let the cakes rest in the oven for 5 minutes and then allow complete cooling before taking them out from the mugs. Garnish with honey just before serving.

Nutrition per Serving

Protein: 6.9g

Fat: 16.3g

Carbohydrate: 2g Net

Orange Marmalade Ice Cream Delight

Total time: 6 hrs

Servings: 6

Ingredients:

- 1½ cup heavy whipping cream

- 2/3 cup orange marmalade

- ¾ cup coconut milk

- 1 tsp vanilla extract

- 2 tbsp erythritol

- Dash of salt

Directions:

Blend all the ingredients in a food processor.

Pour the mixture into ice cream molds and keep in freezer for 6 hours.

Serve chilled.

Nutrition per Serving

Protein: 1.6g

Fat: 22.4g

Carbohydrate: 5.64g Net

Strawberry Flavored Magical Ice Cream

Total time: 4 hrs

Servings: 6

Ingredients:

- ¾ cup Greek yogurt

- 1/3 cup heavy cream

- 3 oz fresh strawberries

- 30 drops vanilla flavoured stevia

- ½ cup coconut milk

Directions:

Put all the ingredients in a food processor and blend them to make a smooth mixture.

Pour the mixture into ice cream molds and keep in freezer for 4 hours. Serve chilled as a desert dish.

Nutrition per Serving

Protein: 1.3g

Fat: 6.4g

Carbohydrate: 4g Net

Yogurt Delight Avocado Ice Cream

Total time: 4 hrs

Servings: 6

Ingredients:

¾ cup Greek yogurt

3 ripe avocados

1/3 cup heavy cream

30 drops vanilla flavoured stevia

½ cup coconut milk

Directions:

Scoop out the avocado flesh and put it in the blender.

Put all the other ingredients in the blender and pulse the device to make a smooth mixture. Pour the mixture into ice cream molds and keep in freezer for four hours.

Serve chilled by garnishing with some avocado slices.

Nutrition per Serving

Protein: 1.3g

Fat: 6.4g

Carbohydrate: 4g Net

Master Blaster Carrot Ice Cream

Total time: 4 hrs

Servings: 6

Ingredients:

¾ cup Greek yogurt

3 medium carrots, grated

1/3 cup whipping cream

30 drops vanilla flavoured stevia

½ cup almond milk

Directions:

Blend all the ingredients in a food processor and pulse the device to make a smooth mixture.

Pour the mixture into six ice cream molds and keep in freezer for four hours.

Serve chilled in ice cream bowls.

Nutrition per Serving

Protein: 1.3g

Fat: 6.4g

Carbohydrate: 4g Net

Butter Delight Toffee Flavored Ice Cream

Total time: 3 hrs

Servings: 12

Ingredients:

1 tsp toffee flavoured liquid stevia

2 cans of coconut milk

½ cup whipping cream

½ cup butter

Directions:

Heat butter in a pan till it turns brown and then put it in a blender.

Put coconut milk, whipping cream, toffee flavoured stevia and coconut milk in the blender and pulse to make a smooth mixture.

Pour the mixture into ice cream molds and keep in freezer for 3 hours. Serve chilled.

Nutrition per Serving

Protein: 3.3g

Fat: 12.3g

Carbohydrate: 3.6g Net

Butter Delight Almond Studded Ice Cream

Total time: 4 hrs

Servings: 12

Ingredients:

 1 tsp almond flavoured liquid stevia

 2 cans of coconut milk

 ½ cup chopped almonds

 ½ cup heavy cream

 ½ cup peanut butter

 ¼ cup almond flakes, for garnishing

Directions:

Heat peanut butter in a pan till it turns golden brown in color and then pour it in a bowl.

Put coconut milk, heavy cream, and liquid stevia in the bowl and use an immersion blender to make a smooth mixture. Not put the chopped almonds into this mixture and distribute them evenly with a spoon.

Pour the mixture into 12 ice cream molds and keep in freezer for four hours. Serve chilled by garnishing with fine almond flakes.

Nutrition per Serving

Protein: 3.3g

Fat: 12.3g

Carbohydrate: 3.6g Net

Triple Melon Magnificent Ice Cream

Total time: 3 hrs

Servings: 8

Ingredients:

1 cup diced honeydew melon, diced

1 cup watermelon, diced

1 cup cantaloupe melon, diced

Juice of 1½ lime

15 drops of stevia

1 cup heavy cream

½ cup coconut milk

Directions:

Put lime juice, coconut milk, heavy cream and stevia in a bowl and use an immersion blender to make smooth mixture.

Now add the melon dices and distribute them evenly with a spoon.

Pour the mixture into ice cream molds and keep in the freezer for 3 hours. Serve chilled.

Nutrition per Serving

Protein: 7.41g

Fat: 3.1g

Carbohydrate: 4.9g Net

Triple Berry Magnificent Ice Cream

Total time: 3 hrs

Servings: 8

Ingredients:

  1 cup blueberries, halved

  1 cup strawberries, cut diced

  1 cup cranberries, halved

  Juice of 1½ lime

  15 drops of stevia

  1 cup heavy cream

  ½ cup coconut milk

Directions:

Put lime juice, coconut milk, heavy cream and stevia in a bowl and use an immersion blender to make smooth mixture.

Now add the berry pieces and distribute them evenly with a spoon.

Pour the mixture into ice cream molds and keep in the freezer for 3 hours. Serve chilled.

Nutrition per Serving

Protein: 7.41g

Fat: 3.1g

Carbohydrate: 4.9g Net

Cheesy Choco-Coffee Ice Cream

Total time: 3 hrs

Servings: 8

Ingredients:

½ cup powdered erythritol

½ tsp vanilla extract

½ cup espresso coffee

8 oz mascarpone cheese

2 tsp cocoa powder

1.5 oz dark chocolate

¾ cup heavy whipping cream

1 tbsp dark rum

Directions:

Chop the chocolate into smaller pieces and mix it with cocoa powder.

Put the cheese in a bowl along with erythritol and beat till the mixture becomes very smooth and then add the heavy cream and vanilla extract. Beat hard to get a smooth mixture.

Now, add the coffee and dark rum to this mixture and stir well. Pour the mixture into ice cream molds and sprinkle the chopped chocolate from top.

Keep in freezer for 3 hours and then serve.

Nutrition per Serving

Protein: 2.9g

Fat: 23.10g

Carbohydrate: 11g Net

Exotic Ice Cream with Flavor of Spice Tea

Total time: 3 hrs 25 mins

Servings: 6

Ingredients:

An inch of fresh ginger

8 cardamom seeds

1 star anise

Pinch of ground cloves

2 cinnamon sticks

2 cups water

½ vanilla bean

2 bags black tea

½ cup almond milk

1.5 cups whipping cream

6 whole peppercorns

¼ cup erythritol

Directions:

Put water, cinnamon stick, vanilla bean, anise, cardamom, ginger, clove and peppercorn in a pan and bring the water to boil. Reduce heat and simmer for next 15 minutes.

Remove the pan from heat, dip the tea bags and let the tea brew for 10 minutes. Strain the spice tea and add the cream and almond milk along with sweetener.

Pour the mixture in ice cream molds and keep in freezer for 3 hours.

Nutrition per Serving

Protein: 2g

Fat: 11g

Carbohydrate: 2g Net

Minty Ice Cream with Bliss of Chocolate

Total time: 5 hrs

Servings: 8

Ingredients:

1½ tsp peppermint extract

1½ tsp arrowroot starch

1 cup heavy cream

1 cup almond milk

1/3 cup unsweetened cocoa powder

A pinch of salt

1/3 cup erythritol

Directions:

Pour the almond milk in a pan and add cream, erythritol, starch, salt and cocoa powder. Whisk thoroughly so that all the ingredients are well mixed. Put the pan on low heat and bring the mixture to boil. Remember to stir continuously. Now remove the pan from heat and add the peppermint extract and then let the mixture to cool down at room temperature.

Pour the mixture into ice cream molds and keep in fridge for 5 hours. Serve by garnishing with some freshly chopped mint leaves and cocoa powder.

Nutrition per Serving

Protein: 3g

Fat: 16g

Carbohydrate: 4.25g Net

Yogurt Ice Cream with Fantastic Matcha Flavor

Total time: 4 hrs 10 mins

Servings: 4

Ingredients:

1 tbsp boiling water

1½ tsp matcha powder

1 tbsp fresh lemon juice

12 oz Greek yogurt

½ cup heavy cream

6 drops stevia extract

1 tsp lemon zest

3 tbsp powdered erythritol

Directions:

Combine the matcha powder with boiling water and keep aside for later use.

Put all the other ingredients in a big bowl and use an immersion blender to make a smooth mixture. Now, pour in the mixture of matcha powder and pulse the blender once again to make the mixture homogeneous.

Pour the mixture into ice cream molds and keep in fridge for 4 hours.

Nutrition per Serving

Protein: 4.9g

Fat: 16g

Carbohydrate: 3.3g Net

Simple Chocolate Flavored Yogurt Ice Cream

Total time: 4 hrs 20 mins

Servings: 12

Ingredients:

2 tbsp cocoa powder

½ cup whipping cream

¼ cup powdered erythritol

25 drops of stevia

½ cup whole milk (vanilla flavoured preferred)

18 oz Greek yogurt

3.5 oz chocolate (finely chopped)

½ tsp vanilla

Directions:

Put a saucepan over medium heat and mix the whipping cream with erythritol, whole milk and cocoa powder. Now add the chocolate pieces and heat till all the pieces melt.

Use a medium bowl to mix the yogurt with stevia and vanilla and then put the chocolate mixture into it. It will be best to use a hand blender here to make a smooth mixture.

Pour the mixture into ice cream molds and keep in fridge for 4 hours. Serve chilled by garnishing with some chocolate flakes.

Nutrition per Serving

Protein: 3g

Fat: 17g

Carbohydrate: 4.9g Net

Almond & Banana Unique Ice Cream (with chia seeds)

Total time: 4 hrs

Servings: 6

Ingredients:

1.5 tbsp chia seeds

½ chopped banana

1/8 tsp vanilla extract

1/8 tsp cinnamon

¾ cup coconut milk

¼ cup whipping cream

½ cup erythritol

Directions:

Put all the ingredients in a food processor and pulse hard to get a smooth paste.

Pour the mixture into ice cream molds and keep in fridge for 4 hours.

Serve chilled by garnishing with some more chia seeds.

Nutrition per Serving

Protein: 3g

Fat: 12g

Carbohydrate: 9g Net

Melon Splendor Creamy Ice Cream

Total time: 4 hrs

Servings: 6

Ingredients:

¾ cup Greek yogurt

1/3 cup heavy cream

3 oz water melon cubes, without seeds

30 drops vanilla flavoured stevia

½ cup coconut milk

Directions:

Put all the ingredients in a food processor and blend them to make a smooth mixture.

Pour the mixture into ice cream molds and keep in freezer for 4 hours. Serve chilled as a desert dish.

Nutrition per Serving

Protein: 1.3g

Fat: 6.4g

Carbohydrate: 4g Net

Roasted Macadamia Nut Ice Cream

Total time: 4 hrs

Servings: 6

Ingredients:

¾ cup Greek yogurt

1/3 cup heavy cream

2 cups roasted Macadamia nuts

30 drops vanilla flavoured stevia

½ cup coconut milk

Directions:

Put all the ingredients in a food processor and blend them to make a smooth mixture.

Pour the mixture into ice cream molds and keep in freezer for 4 hours. Serve chilled as a desert dish by garnishing with some Macadamia nut flakes.

Nutrition per Serving

Protein: 1.3g

Fat: 6.4g

Carbohydrate: 4g Net

Magical Coffee Ice Cream Bars with Almond Crust

Total time: 3 hrs 30 mins

Servings: 12

Ingredients:

2 tbsp gelatine

3 cups full fat coconut milk

1 tsp instant espresso coffee powder

½ cup erythritol

3 egg yolks

2 oz sugar free chocolate

½ tsp vanilla extract

1 cup finely chopped almonds

Directions:

Use a saucepan to add the gelatine with ½ cup coconut milk and allow 3 minutes of standing time. Then heat the mixture so that the gelatine dissolves.

Now add the remaining coconut milk along with sweetener and coffee powder and stir till every ingredient is dissolved.

Whisk the egg yolks in a bowl and add it slowly to the mixture in saucepan, allowing enough time to temper the egg yolk. Cook for some time and then place the mixture in a cold bath to bring the temperature down.

Pour the mixture into ice cream molds and keep in fridge for 3 hours.

In the mean time melt the chocolate on double boiler and as the ice cream is set, dip the bars in chocolate followed by rolling them over the flaked almonds and return them to fridge for another 20 minutes.

Nutrition per Serving

Protein: 3.83g

Fat: 21.6g

Carbohydrate: 6.03g Net

Chocolate Ice Cream Bars with Blueberry Coating

Total time: 3 hrs 30 mins

Servings: 12

Ingredients:

2 tbsp gelatine

3 cups full fat coconut milk

1 tsp instant espresso coffee powder

½ cup erythritol

3 egg yolks

2 oz sugar free chocolate

½ tsp vanilla extract

1 cup chopped blueberries

Directions:

Use a saucepan to add the gelatine with ½ cup coconut milk and allow 3 minutes of standing time. Then heat the mixture so that the gelatine dissolves. Now, add the remaining coconut milk along with sweetener and coffee powder and stir till every ingredient is dissolved. Whisk the egg yolks in a bowl and add it slowly to the mixture in saucepan, allowing enough time to temper the egg yolk. Cook for some time and then place the mixture in a cold bath to bring the temperature down.

Pour the mixture into ice cream molds and keep in fridge for 3 hours. In the mean time melt the chocolate on double boiler and as the ice cream is set, dip the bars in chocolate followed by rolling them over the chopped berries. Place the ice cream bars on a baking sheet and return them to fridge for another 20 minutes.

Nutrition per Serving

Protein: 3.83g

Fat: 21.6g

Carbohydrate: 8.3g Net

Ice Cream with Rich Cheese and Berries

Total time: 4 hrs

Servings: 6

Ingredients:

- ½ tsp vanilla extract

- ½ cup plain Greek yogurt

- 8 oz heavy cream cheese

- ½ cup almond milk

- 1½ cup cranberries

- ¼ cup powdered erythritol

Directions:

Put all the ingredients in a food processor and pulse to make a smooth paste.

Pour the mixture into ice cream molds and keep in freezer for 4 hours. Serve in ice cream bowls by garnishing with sliced cranberries.

Nutrition per Serving

Protein: 6g

Fat: 7g

Carbohydrate: 8g Net

Cheesy Yogurt Ice Cream with Mango Pulp

Total time: 4 hrs

Servings: 6

Ingredients:

½ tsp vanilla extract

½ cup plain Greek yogurt

8 oz heavy cream cheese

½ cup almond milk

1½ cup mashed ripe mangoes

¼ cup powdered erythritol

Directions:

Put all the ingredients in a food processor and pulse to make a smooth paste.

Pour the mixture into ice cream molds and keep in freezer for 4 hours. Serve in ice cream bowls by garnishing with freshly sliced mangoes.

Nutrition per Serving

Protein: 6g

Fat: 7g

Carbohydrate: 9g Net

Cool Lemon & Buttermilk Ice Cream

Total time: 3 hrs

Servings: 6

Ingredients:

¼ tsp stevia glycerite

1 cup almond milk

1 cup heavy cream

1 cup buttermilk

A pinch of salt

2 tbsp lemon juice

Zest of one lemon

½ cup erythritol

Directions:

Put all the ingredients in a food processor and pulse for a couple of minutes to make a smooth mixture.

Pour the mixture into ice cream molds and keep in freezer 3 hours.

Nutrition per Serving

Protein: 1g

Fat: 6g

Carbohydrate: 1g Net

Buttermilk & Avocado Delight Ice Cream

Total time: 3 hrs

Servings: 6

Ingredients:

¼ tsp stevia glycerite

1 cup almond milk

1 cup heavy cream

1 cup buttermilk

A pinch of salt

3 ripe avocados

1 avocado, diced

½ cup erythritol

Directions:

Scoop out the flesh of the avocado and then put all the ingredients in a food processor and pulse for a couple of minutes to make a smooth mixture. Now, add the avocado dices into the mixture and use a spoon to distribute them evenly.

Pour the mixture into ice cream molds and keep in freezer 3 hours.

Nutrition per Serving

Protein: 1g

Fat: 6g

Carbohydrate: 3g Net

Buttermilk Magic Muskmelon Ice Cream

Total time: 3 hrs

Servings: 6

Ingredients:

¼ tsp stevia glycerite

1 cup almond milk

1 cup heavy cream

1 cup buttermilk

A pinch of salt

3 cups mashed muskmelon

1 cup muskmelon cubes

5 drops melon essence

½ cup erythritol

Directions:

Put all the ingredients (except the melon cubes) in a food processor and pulse for a couple of minutes to make a smooth mixture. Now, add the melon cubes into the mixture and distribute them evenly.

Pour the mixture into ice cream molds and keep in freezer 3 hours.

Nutrition per Serving

Protein: 1g

Fat: 6g

Carbohydrate: 8g Net

Delightful Double Berry Buttery Ice Cream

Total time: 4 hrs 10 mins

Servings: 6

Ingredients:

¼ tsp stevia glycerite

1 cup almond milk

1 cup heavy cream

1 cup buttermilk

¼ cup melted butter

A pinch of salt

3 cups mashed strawberries

1 cup mashed blueberry

5 drops berry essence

½ cup erythritol

Directions:

Put all the ingredients stevia glycerite, almond milk, heavy cream, buttermilk, melted butter, salt, and erythritol in the food processor and pulse for a minute.

Now divide the mixture into 2 bowls ((divide it in 1:3 proportion). Keep the larger portion in the food processor, add the mashed strawberries along with 3 drops of berry essence and then pulse once again to make the mixture smooth. Pour this mixture into ice cream molds (they must not be entirely filled with the ice cream mixture as you will have to add the blueberry layer later) and keep in freezer 2 hours.

Now add the mashed blueberries along with the remaining berry essence with the rest portion of creamy mixture and let it chill for 30 minutes in the freezer. Bring out the ice cream molds from the freezer and then pour the blueberry layer over the top. Take the molds back to the freezer and let the ice creams set. This will take two more hours.

Serve chilled by garnishing with some freshly chopped berries.

Nutrition per Serving

Protein: 1.9g

Fat: 6g

Carbohydrate: 10g Net

Peach Fantasy Buttery Ice Cream

Total time: 3 hrs

Servings: 6

Ingredients:

¼ tsp stevia glycerite

1 cup almond milk

1 cup heavy cream

1 cup buttermilk

A pinch of salt

3 cups mashed peach

1 cup peach cubes

2 drops peach essence

½ cup erythritol

Directions:

Put all the ingredients (except the peach cubes) in a food processor and pulse for a couple of minutes to make a smooth mixture. Now, add the peach cubes into the mixture and distribute them evenly.

Pour the mixture into ice cream molds and keep in freezer 3 hours.

Nutrition per Serving

Protein: 1g

Fat: 6g

Carbohydrate: 7g Net

Lemon & Berry Double Twist Ice Cream

Total time: 3 hrs

Servings: 6

Ingredients:

¼ tsp stevia glycerite

1 cup almond milk

1 cup heavy cream

1 cup buttermilk

A pinch of salt

3 cups mashed strawberries

1 tbsp lemon juice

1 cup lemon cubes

2 drops lemon essence

¾ cup erythritol

Directions:

Put all the ingredients (except the lemon cubes) in a food processor and pulse for a couple of minutes to make a smooth mixture. Now, add the lemon cubes into the mixture and distribute them evenly.

Pour the mixture into ice cream molds and keep in freezer 3 hours.

Nutrition per Serving

Protein: 1g

Fat: 6g

Carbohydrate: 6g Net

Rich Coconut Splendor Ice Cream

Total time: 3 hrs

Servings: 6

Ingredients:

¼ tsp stevia glycerite

1 cup coconut milk

1 cup heavy cream

1 cup buttermilk

A pinch of salt

3 cups coconut flakes

1 tsp coconut essence

¾   cup erythritol

Directions:

Put all the ingredients (except the coconut flakes) in a food processor and pulse for a couple of minutes to make a smooth mixture. Now, add the coconut flakes into the mixture and distribute them evenly.

Pour the mixture into ice cream molds and keep in freezer 3 hours.

Nutrition per Serving

Protein: 1g

Fat: 6g

Carbohydrate: 9g Net

Buttery Coffee Ice Cream

Total time: 3 hrs

Servings: 6

Ingredients:

¼ tsp stevia glycerite

1 cup whole milk

1 cup heavy whipping cream

1 cup buttermilk

A pinch of salt

2 tbsp cocoa powder

1 tsp instant coffee granules

¾   cup erythritol

Directions:

Put cocoa powder, melted butter, and coffee granules in a bowl and blend them thoroughly.

Now, put all the ingredients along with the buttery coffee mixture in a food processor and pulse for a couple of minutes to make a smooth mixture.

Pour the mixture into ice cream molds and keep in freezer 3 hours.

Nutrition per Serving

Protein: 1g

Fat: 6g

Carbohydrate: 1g Net

Fudgy Almond Magical Ice Cream

Total time: 3 hrs

Servings: 5

Ingredients:

1 cup unsweetened almond milk

1 cup unsweetened coconut milk

2½ tbsp unsweetened cocoa powder

2 tbsp raw & unsweetened coconut butter

2 tbsp chocolate chips

1½ tbsp coconut flakes

2½ tbsp honey

½ tsp almond extract

Directions:

Put all the ingredients in a food processor and blend them to make a smooth mixture.

Pour the mixture into ice cream molds and keep in freezer for 3 hours.

Nutrition per Serving

Protein: 2g

Fat: 12g

Carbohydrate: 3.1g Net

Duet of Avocado & Lime

Total time: 4 hrs

Servings: 6

Ingredients:

  Peel of one lime

  2 large ripe avocados

  Juice of 2 limes

  ½ cup erythritol

  2 cups coconut milk

  1 cup whipping cream

  20 drops liquid stevia

Directions:

Cut the avocadoes and throw away the seeds. Now, scoop out the flesh and put it in food processor along with all other ingredients.

Pulse the food processor to make a smooth mixture.

Pour the mixture into ice cream molds and keep in freezer for four hours. Serve chilled.

Nutrition per Serving

Protein: 2.9g

Fat: 25.9g

Carbohydrate: 5.3g Net

Coconut & Cranberry Ice Cream

Total time: 3 hrs

Servings: 4

Ingredients:

¾ cup fresh cranberries

½ cup coconut milk

2 tbsp chia seeds

½ cup unsweetened almond milk

¾ cup heavy cream

8 drops stevia

1 tbsp shredded coconut (unsweetened)

Directions:

Put all the ingredients in a food processor and pulse the device to make a smooth mixture.

Pour the mixture into ice cream molds and keep in freezer for 3 hours. Serve chilled by garnishing with some more shredded coconut.

Nutrition per Serving

Protein: 1.8g

Fat: 5g

Carbohydrate: 6.8g Net

Hidden Mango Delight Inside Super Chocolate

Total time: 5 hrs 15 mins

Servings: 4

Ingredients for making ice cream:

1 tbsp erythritol

½ tsp mango extract

1 cup heavy whipping cream

2 cups ripe mango pulp

½ cup ripe mango cubes (frozen)

Ingredients for making chocolate shell:

1 tbsp erythritol

¾ cup coconut oil

3 tbsp heavy whipping cream

1 oz baking chocolate (unsweetened)

1 tbsp cocoa powder

Directions:

Put all the ice cream making ingredients (except mango cubes) in a bowl and use a hand blender to make smooth paste. Now, add the mango cubes and distribute them evenly with a spoon. Pour this paste into ice cream molds and keep in freezer for at least 5 hours.

In order to make the chocolate shell, the chocolate is to be melted in a saucepan and then add the other ingredients. Stir till the chocolate melts and all ingredients dissolve in it.

Bring out the ice creams from the molds and dip into the liquid chocolate mixture. Allow 15 seconds of standing time so that the shell can become hard and then take them back to freezer for another 15 minutes.

Nutrition per Serving

Protein: 3g

Fat: 37g

Carbohydrate: 3.8g Net

Coconut Blast Inside Dark Chocolate

Total time: 5 hrs 15 mins

Servings: 4

Ingredients for making ice cream:

  1 tbsp erythritol

  ½ tsp coconut essence

  1 cup heavy whipping cream

  2 cups shredded coconut

  ½ cup coconut flesh, cut into cubes

Ingredients for making chocolate shell:

  1 tbsp erythritol

  ¾ cup coconut oil

  3 tbsp heavy whipping cream

  1 oz dark chocolate (unsweetened)

  1 tbsp cocoa powder

Directions:

Put all the ice cream making ingredients (except cubes of coconut flesh) in a bowl and use a hand blender to make smooth paste. Now, add the coconut cubes and distribute them evenly with a spoon. Pour this paste into ice cream molds and keep in freezer for at least 5 hours.

In order to make the chocolate shell, the chocolate is to be melted in a saucepan and then add the other ingredients. Stir till the chocolate melts and all ingredients dissolve in it.

Bring out the ice creams from the molds and dip into the liquid chocolate mixture. Allow 15 seconds of standing time so that the shell can become hard and then take them back to freezer for another 15 minutes.

Nutrition per Serving

Protein: 3g

Fat: 37g

Carbohydrate: 4g Net

Very Berry Choco Magic

Total time: 5 hrs 15 mins

Servings: 4

Ingredients for making ice cream:

1 tbsp erythritol

½ tsp strawberry extract

1 cup heavy whipping cream

2 cups mashed strawberries

½ cup diced strawberries

Ingredients for making chocolate shell:

1 tbsp erythritol

¾ cup coconut oil

3 tbsp heavy whipping cream

1 oz baking chocolate (unsweetened)

1 tbsp cocoa powder

Directions:

Put all the ice cream making ingredients (except strawberry dices) in a bowl and use a hand blender to make smooth paste. Now, add the strawberry pieces and distribute them evenly with a spoon. Pour this paste into ice cream molds and keep in freezer for at least 5 hours.

In order to make the chocolate shell, the chocolate is to be melted in a saucepan and then add the other ingredients. Stir till the chocolate melts and all ingredients dissolve in it.

Bring out the ice creams from the molds and dip into the liquid chocolate mixture. Allow 15 seconds of standing time so that the shell can become hard and then take them back to freezer for another 15 minutes.

Nutrition per Serving

Protein: 3g

Fat: 37g

Carbohydrate: 3.2g Net

Kiwi Delight Dipped in White Chocolate

Total time: 5 hrs 15 mins

Servings: 4

Ingredients for making ice cream:

   1 tbsp erythritol

   ½ tsp kiwi fruit extract

   1 cup heavy whipping cream

   2 cups mashed kiwi fruit

   ½ cup diced kiwi fruit

Ingredients for making chocolate shell:

   1 tbsp erythritol

   ¾ cup coconut oil

   3 tbsp heavy whipping cream

   1 oz white chocolate powder (unsweetened)

   1 tsp chocolate essence

Directions:

Put all the ice cream making ingredients (except kiwi dices) in a bowl and use a hand blender to make smooth paste. Now, add the kiwi fruit pieces and distribute them evenly with a spoon. Pour this paste into ice cream molds and keep in freezer for at least 5 hours.

In order to make the chocolate shell, the chocolate is to be blended with all other ingredients. Stir till the chocolate melts and all ingredients dissolve in it.

Bring out the ice creams from the molds and dip into the liquid chocolate mixture. Allow 15 seconds of standing time so that the shell can become hard and then take them back to freezer for another 15 minutes.

Nutrition per Serving

Protein: 3g

Fat: 37g

Carbohydrate: 3.7g Net

Made in the USA
Lexington, KY
16 January 2017